Ryuho OKAWA Grand Messiah Hypothesis

Ryuho OKAWA Grand Messiah Hypothesis
First edition：August, 2018
Author：Kunihiko Kakoi
Publisher：TriboLogics Corporation
Address：〒110-0016 402 ParkGrandy,
3-31-4 Taito, Taito-ku, Tokyo, Japan
TEL：81-3-5816-3590, FAX：81-3-5816-3591
E-mail：info@tribology.co.jp
http://www.tribology.co.jp
Printing and Bookbinding：Sanbi Corporation

©Kunihiko Kakoi 2018, Printed in Japan,
ISBN978-4-904176-04-7

Ryuho OKAWA Grand Messiah Hypothesis

Table of Contents

1. Preface	1
2. Ryuho OKAWA Spiritual Messages	7
3. Messages from Maitreya the Christ	31
4. The Prophecies of Michel Nostradamus	47
5. Miracles within the Happy Science	61
6. Conclusion	67

1. Preface

The heliocentric Copernican theory brought revolutionary changes to the understanding of the universe and the Earth. The worldview has been changed from the geocentric way of thinking to the heliocentric view. The heliocentric theory explained well many phenomena based on a few assumptions. But it had taken many years before the theory became commonly accepted, involving unfortunate incidences such as the trial of Galileo. Today hardly anybody doubts the heliocentric theory.

The continental drift theory advanced by Alfred Wegener brought revolutionary changes to the understanding of the continents and the continental movements. Until then, it was hardly conceivable that large continents move and drift. It is said that the British philosopher Francis Bacon and other persons in the Age of Great Voyages were the first to point out that the contour line of the western side of the African Continent and that of the eastern side of South America curiously coincides.

After that a phenomenon had been found where some fossils were common on both sides of the continents, and to explain it Alfred Wegener announced that the continents had originally been one and thereafter it had been divided into two continents. It is said he also offered many other circumstantial evidences, for instance the coincidence of the strata of both continents and the polar wander paths. Up until then, there had even been a hypothesis contending that there were land bridges connecting both continents to explain the phenomenon of common fossils.

Although Wegener's continental drift theory had explained well these phenomena, it took years before it would become commonly accepted. It is said that he had been ridiculed from many academics because the explanation of the force that causes the continental drift was not adequate. But thanks to other phenomena such as the ocean-floor spreading having been discovered, Wegener's continental drift theory was finally fully accepted. Today hardly anybody doubts the continental drift theory. Now we can observe the drifting velocity of the continents using GPS. There are many articles on this topic in Wikipedia.

We can see from these considerations that if a hypothesis explains independent phenomena consistently and there are no other hypotheses which can explain the phenomena well, then a hypothesis must be regarded as the presently established truth.

Now, here we have four independent phenomena. To explain these phenomena, I am putting forth the "Ryuho OKAWA Grand Messiah Hypothesis".

⑴　Ryuho OKAWA Spiritual Messages

Master Ryuho OKAWA had spiritually awakened unexpectedly on March 23, 1981. From that moment on, he had been receiving spiritual messages from Jesus Christ and other great men in the history of the world. The messages are full of truth and that in itself indicates that Master OKAWA is the Grand Messiah. Master OKAWA had founded in Japan the religious group Happy Science in 1986. (http://happy-science.org/)

(2) Messages from Maitreya the Christ

"Messages from Maitreya the Christ" are 140 spiritual messages which Mr. Benjamin Creme, British artist and esotericist, had received from Maitreya in Heaven in a period from September 6, 1977 to May 27, 1982. In these Messages, Maitreya reveals that He had descended from Heaven and is now dwelling in our world. And also He reveals the necessity of a drastic change of the world to realize a Utopia in our world. The messages are full of reality. The group "Share International", founded by Mr. Benjamin Creme, is independent of the religious group Happy Science. I want to especially point to the fact that the date March 23, 1981 when Master OKAWA had spiritually awakened is included in the period in which Maitreya had given His 140 messages. It is supposed that Maitreya in Heaven himself as its overall manager had brought the spiritual awakening of Master Ryuho OKAWA.

(Share International : http://www.share-international.org/)

(3) The Prophecies of Michel Nostradamus

I have interpreted some prophecies of Nostradamus related to the Grand Messiah from his original French text. A famous prophecy of the 7th month 1999 (10.72) can be interpreted as that the Grand Messiah would descend at the end of the 20th century. Another prophecy of Hermes (10.75) can be interpreted that the Grand Messiah would descend in Asia. Hermes is said to be one of the previous incarnations of Master Ryuho OKAWA. These two Prophecies indicate the time and the place the Grand Messiah would descend. And also in the prophecy (5.53), the word "The law of the Sun" appears explicitly, which is the title of one of the foundational books by Master OKAWA. This prophecy can be interpreted that the Sun (Japan) would retain the Law of the Grand Messiah. It is speculated that the ultimate purpose of the prophecies of Nostradamus is to predict the advent of the Grand Messiah.

(4)　Miracles within the Happy Science

Now within the Happy Science, many miracles are reported that have left medical professionals astonished. And also, other channelers besides Master OKAWA exist who can channel spiritual messages. Whether it be an angel or a devil, there is no spirit whom Master OKAWA cannot summon. Master OKAWA invites any spirit into the channeler and lets him speak and lets him return. The words of the summoned spirits are full of truth.

These independent four phenomena focus on the singular point that Master Ryuho OKAWA is the Grand Messiah. It would certainly be the work of a heavenly miracle and a magnificent story designed by Heaven.

The basis of physics is hypothesis. Any hypothesis is allowed whenever it explains given phenomena consistently. A simple hypothesis is preferable. As in the early days of Wegener's continental drift theory, at present we cannot say that the Ryuho OKAWA Grand Messiah hypothesis is accepted as common knowledge.

It is said that in physics, anyone must be able to repeat and verify a given phenomenon. For spiritual phenomena too, it seems that anyone can repeat and verify a given phenomenon, if he sufficiently accumulates spiritual training. It is the same as when elementary school students cannot repeat and verify the Michelson-Morley experiment that indicates the constancy of the speed of light. Unless they study mathematics and physics, they cannot repeat and verify the experiment.

In the following, I will explain the four phenomena in detail based on the Ryuho OKAWA Grand Messiah hypothesis. I decided that the reader should be able to read through this article without referring to other documents. As a result, I beg for the reader's pardon for the lengthiness of this article. Statements referred from other documents are in MS Reference Sans Serif.

Furthermore, I am a member of the religious group Happy Science, so in my high regard for Master OKAWA I must ask for my reader's patience, but I shall not let it affect the logic of my argument.

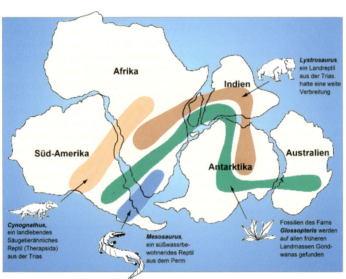

From Wikipedia file Gondwana fossil map ger.png

2. Ryuho OKAWA Spiritual Messages

Master Ryuho OKAWA had spiritually awakened unexpectedly on March 23, 1981. For us modern people, it may not be easy to believe, but from that moment on he had the ability to converse with heavenly spirits. We are taught that until then he was an office worker not all that different from us.

The volume of messages, which Master OKAWA had received from heavenly spirits, Jesus Christ and other great men from the history of the world, are enormous. The messages had been published successively since the latter half of the 1980s. Currently these are collected in the books as "Ryuho OKAWA Spiritual Messages" (published from the religious group Happy Science). Here I want to introduce some messages from successively published books, which have left a great impression on me. It may be that not only are the contents interesting of course, but also differences in the speaker's personalities may be felt.

The following message was given from an old Japanese Buddhist Nichiren, now in heaven, to a questioner who had been suffering from spiritual disability. In this message, Nichiren teaches us that man's life is a book of problems.

Spiritual Messages of Nichiren, Chobunsha,
Editorial author : Saburo YOSHIKAWA, August 15, 1985,
Channeler : Ryuho OKAWA, p.49,
(Translated from Japanese to English by K.Kakoi)

Questioner : It might be so, but even in the case of a teacher in the human world, even if he is free, if a student does not study and spends all his time in idle amusement, the teacher would scold him and in some cases he would forcibly take the student back to the classroom, grabbing his arms and force him to sit at his seat. Nevertheless you guardian spirits and guiding spirits would leave him to act freely. Even though I dare not say that you are irresponsible, is that not merciless of you, even if God had given us freedom.

Nichiren : I want you to understand that we are not here to give you the solutions in advance. Man's life is a book of problems. Each man must solve his book of problems with strenuous effort. We of course have the solution and know the answer. But do you think it is good for a student to be taught the answer easily? Man's life is a book of problems. Can we teach him the solution? It depends on his progress too. If a student who has almost reached the solution wants a little hint, we may give him it. But we cannot give him the answer when he has no basis of study or he makes no efforts to solve the problems. Because to do so is utterly missing the original objective of your life on Earth. Can you understand?

We have the solution. We can give you the solution. But the act offers no good results to your life on Earth. Man's life is a book of problems. The solutions and your exam records are revealed after you have died and returned to our world. In this way, the system is designed.

Here it is taught that if a man wants to have no anguishes and no problems in his life, it is the same as if he had wanted to have no problems printed on his book of problems. Also it is taught that a man who has much anguish and many problems is a man who is expected to fight with the problems and to solve them and to make great achievements in its process. If the problems encountered in our life are the problems written in our book of problems, then we may have room to see them objectively.

The next spiritual message is the one given from Master Tendai Chigi who is an old Chinese Buddhist now in heaven and teaches the concept of Heaven and Hell.

Spiritual Messages of Kukai, Chobunsha,
Editorial author : Saburo YOSHIKAWA, November 15, 1985,
Channeler : Ryuho OKAWA, p.90
(Translated from Japanese to English by K.Kakoi)

Questioner : In conclusion, you say that the world outside of this earthly realm can roughly be divided into two worlds?

Chigi : Yes. But rather than thinking of it as Heaven and Hell, it is better to think of it as someone who is healthy and someone who is sick. If there are patients suffering from diseases and if you think that these persons must be killed, that would be a dangerous thought. This is what I am talking about.

Persons who are sick must enter a hospital for a period until they get well. And then they are expected to return to a healthy state. Of course there is nothing wrong with hospitals. Any healthy person might get ill. So I do not want you to think in dualistic terms, that there are heavenly spirits and evil spirits. There are times when people are well and there are times when people are sick. It is not that there are healthy types of people, anymore than there are people who are of the sick type. People should in fact be healthy. But there are times when people will get sick, you must understand.

Diseases require treatment and a certain period to be cured. So from now on when you think of hell, I do not want you to think that there are evil spirits, evil people, or denizens of hell. I want you to think of them as sick patients. To God, both healthy and sick persons are children of God. People who are sick are not bad. Therefore, when you think of evil spirits, think of them as patients who are sick. They may be sick at the moment, but they are originally healthy persons. When people get sick they might complain and say foolish things. When people are sick and full of discontent they can only think of themselves. Surely you can understand this.

The reason why evil spirits are greedy and selfish and are dominated by them is because they are sick patients. Take a look at patients who are sick in hospitals. They can only think about themselves. They are thinking only about how to overcome their disease. They can only think about how they might free themselves from pain, all the great food they would like to eat, where they might want to go if they recovered. That is because they are truly sick. And I want you to see that. —Therefore, think not that there are these types of people who are sick, but that healthy people can become sick, and that sick people may recover. This is how you should see it.

According to the Christian vision of hell, if a person goes to hell he cannot be saved. But the vision of hell depicted here is very different from that. It is stated here that hell is a God-given Mercy. This vision of hell has the potential for hope and salvation.

The following spiritual message was given by Ameno Minakanushi no Mikoto, a Central Japanese Shinto God, speaking on religious truth.

Spiritual Messages of Amaterasu Ohmikami, Chobunsha,
Editorial author : Saburo YOSHIKAWA, March 15, 1986,
Channeler : Ryuho OKAWA, p.126
(Translated from Japanese to English by K.Kakoi)

Questioner : It seems to me that even as ultimately there is only the monism of the light, this being the true state of humans, it is also true that in this three dimensional world people are drawn to the darkness and are suffering.

Minakanushi : This is precisely why we must emphasize the "monism of the light". As long as man thinks there is the light and then there is the darkness, he shall not find salvation. When he believes that there is only the light, then from that moment on he has the chance to be saved.

All of you will probably experience sickness during your lives. Now, if you believe that your sickness comes from God, shall you recover from your sickness? It would be extremely difficult indeed. This sickness is not from God. God does not create sickness. As you believe this you will find the energy, the courage, the confidence to overcome your sickness.

The aim of religion would not be only to explain facts objectively. Religion saves man, and gives him the strength to stand. It is something that gives man a perspective on life. Religion does not merely report the condition of humanity, like observing a bunch of ants. It is the essence of religion to teach man the true state of his being, how to live and to be redeemed!

If this is true, then recognize that religious truth is not the same as the truth of observing things with a magnifying glass. Religious truth is not about "what is," but about "what ought to be".

It is because we only see "what is", that we think there is good and there is evil, there is the light and then there is the darkness. When the truth of "what ought to be" is seen, then darkness just does not exist, and there is no such thing as sickness. Such things do not exist in "what ought to be".

It is a question of the difference in standpoints on how you see this truth. From the standpoint of religion there can be nothing but the singularity of goodness and the monism of the light. If you wish to explain what is, then you are free to do so. But religious truth is singular.

I was impressed by the fact that the god who is at the center of Japanese Shintoism has such monism of the light as stated here. He states it strongly that humans are children of God, a bundle of hope. It seems that spiritual messages from gods of Japanese Shintoism especially has an uplifting and healing effect on people. It is said that Master Masaharu Taniguchi, the leader of a Japanese religious group called Seicho-no-ie (Home of Growth) has healed many people through the guidance and power of Ameno Minakanushi no Mikoto.

Next, I want to present the spiritual messages from Kaishu KATSU who had played an important role in the Meiji Restoration.

Spiritual Messages of Ryoma SAKAMOTO, Chobunsha,
Editorial author : Saburo YOSHIKAWA, July 25, 1986,
Channeler : Ryuho OKAWA, p.137
(Translated from Japanese to English by K.Kakoi)

Questioner : For the purpose of heightening our awareness
on these matters, can you explain to us about, for example,
why it is that even as the guidance from spirits from heaven
have been made repeatedly of the true spiritual nature of
man, once he is born in this world as flesh he soon forgets
his past?

KATSU : Well, different priests probably will give you all sorts
of different answers on this matter, but if you ask me, it is
like a school play. If you go to a school play you will see kids
playing a princess or maybe a prince. Very good. It is good
because you are completely in your role as prince, or a
princess, or maybe even a knight or a warrior. If you are
thinking about what grade you are in and which class you
come from, and how you might not be good at math but all
right in English, well then you will not be able to take part in
the play. Just think of it as a school play, all you have to do
is play the part completely. There is something you can take
back from the play after it is over. Oh, that knight was played
well, or hey that princess was nice, or that prince was good.
That is all very good. There is no need to think about what
grade or which class you are in, or what your name is, or

how you might have had an argument with your parents, or how much allowance money you have. It is just like this. You do not have to know anything. That is why it is fun.

KATSU explains the relationship about this world and the next in a simple way that is different from the religionists. It reminds one of the style that can be seen in "Hikawa Seiwa" (Quiet talks at the Hikawa mansion). It is said that the Meiji Restoration is a great achievement by the Bodhisattvas who were born in Japan together all at once.

Next, I want to present the spiritual message from Moses of the Old Testament. He tells us that the present day is the age of the Rebirth of Buddha. He also tells that the present day is the age of crisis but also the age of hopes.

New Spiritual Teachings from Moses, IRH press,
Author : Ryuho OKAWA, March 20, 1989, p.209
(Translated from Japanese to English by K.Kakoi)

The Rebirth of Buddha

  I have been talking about various methodologies up until
now, but I wish here to express my own perspective. It is
about recognizing this modern age. It is about a new
recognition for modern people. It is about the recognition of
a new worldview. It is about a new awareness of the times.
It is about realizing that this age is the age of the rebirth of
Buddha. This era is of such times.

  Formerly Shakyamuni was born in India and there was an
age of true dharma. Then came the age of replicated
dharma, and then the age of obsolete dharma, and now once
again the age of true dharma is dawning. You must
understand that you are living in such an age when Buddha
is reborn. You must understand that Buddha has been reborn
in a country in the East and in that country new truths are
being revealed. With these new truths at the helm you must
realize that such guiding spirit has arrived upon the Earth.

  As I have once worked miracles in the land of Egypt, as
Jesus had once worked miracles in Israel, henceforth such
holy miracles shall manifest in various forms. And people

2. Ryuho OKAWA Spiritual Messages

shall eventually realize the meaning of this age, the true scale of its meaning. This is because this age is moving in accordance with the greater design of a vast God. In this age a big star of the savior shines. This star emerges upon the Earth once every two thousand, maybe three thousand years. This star is now shining upon the Earth. And this star is shining brighter, more powerfully than ever.

This is because the life that has been reborn in the East is emitting a degree of force and scale of mission hitherto never manifested. And the people must understand that this rebirth of Buddha is the kernel of Buddha. They must understand the true magnitude of the meaning of the emergence of the kernel of Buddha. This manifestation of the kernel of Buddha upon this Earth is a rare occasion. They must realize that the kernel of Buddha has emerged. It is because only with such great power can a great many people be saved. Only with such great power can all of the regions be saved.

In Israel Jesus taught the truth. Perhaps he was able to save many Israelis. However, it took two thousand years of history for the teachings of Jesus to envelop the world. Perhaps Buddha was able to save many Indians, but it took a very long time for his teachings to spread to the rest of the world.

However in this era of ours, we can not be so lax. Humanity is facing a crisis. People do not recognize this. They do not understand that humanity is facing a crisis. They believe that just as they had yesterday, they have today, and just as they have today they will have a tomorrow. However there is no tomorrow. Unless humanity mends itself and begins to create the world of the divine, there is no tomorrow. This is the truth of this era. This is the danger we face. The people must know about this.

Unless the land of the divine, the land of Buddha is built now, a new light of hope for humanity will not come. This era is of such great magnitude. Understand this. Great forces are gathering for this purpose. Understand this. You must understand this. To understand this is to understand the ultimate secret. It is the ultimate key to understanding the secret of our age. This is the key to unlocking the purpose of modern Japan.

People, do not waste your time in idleness. Do not live in idleness. The age of great transformation is upon us. Can you understand why we are sending you spiritual messages to the Earth with rapid succession? Can you understand why we are transmitting spiritual messages continuously? Why are we transmitting spiritual messages continuously like this? Has such a thing ever happened before? Has such a thing ever even taken place once? Has anything like this ever happened on Earth? Have all of the guiding spirits of heaven sent spiritual messages together at once like this before? In

2. Ryuho OKAWA Spiritual Messages

which religion has such a thing happened before? In the history of which modern people are aware, such a thing has never taken place.

The highest guiding spirits of heaven are successively transmitting their own thoughts to people directly because humanity has already entered a time of extreme trials. There is no other way to save humanity than to establish upon the Earth the tower of light, the tower of truth and to fill the Earth with the light of truth and to make the kingdom of God upon the Earth.

Soon a vast darkness will cover the Earth, cover the people of Earth. There will come a time when the darkness will be overwhelming and the people will lose hope. A land of light will be needed in such times. We need the light. A light from the lighthouse is needed. We need light that shines on people, that shines in the darkness. This is why we are doing this. Understand the immensity of what this means.

We too are working restlessly. Understand why we are working so restlessly. We are creating the land of truth. To build the land of God, to expand the land of God, to establish the kingdom of God is sought after. The kingdom of God must be established before the darkness completely swallows up the world. A Utopia must be built. The land of Buddha must be created. Unless that is built, there is no tomorrow for humanity. The time has come for this. We are trying to build a house of light. It is a necessity.

This modern age is the age of the grand messiah, and even as it is the age of great peril, it is also the age of great hope. We feel the weight of the words of Moses.

Finally I want to present the spiritual message from Master Masaharu TANIGUCHI who in his lifetime founded the Japanese religious group "Seicho-no-Ie".

(http://www.seicho-no-ie.org/eng/)

Great Resurrection of Masaharu TANIGUCHI, Tsuchiya Shoten, Author : Ryuho OKAWA, August 20, 1988, p.240
(Translated from Japanese to English by K.Kakoi)

Understand that victory or defeat is already decided by the fact. Only Masaharu TANIGUCHI himself can speak the "Spiritual Messages of Masaharu TANIGUCHI". Nobody else on Earth can transmit the contents of my spiritual messages as I do. Only Masaharu TANIGUCHI can transmit it. Even as there is a book entitled "Great Resurrection of Masaharu TANIGUCHI", it is only Masaharu TANIGUCHI who can speak on the resurrection. Whether that is true or not, the fact of the matter itself had already been decided. The fact itself decides victory or defeat.

So you who believe in this dharma, have no doubt. Be strong and firm. The fact itself decides victory or defeat.

Master Masaharu TANIGUCHI says that Masaharu TANIGUCHI himself is speaking from heaven, so it cannot be doubted. The fact decides the victory or defeat. Indeed, such a strong and confident speech can only be made by the man himself.

Hitherto presented spiritual messages of "gods" are full of strength and originality, which can only be imparted by the real deal.

Here, I want to quote from his book on the circumstances that surrounded Master OKAWA when he had gotten his spiritual awakening.

"THE LAWS OF THE SUN" Ryuho OKAWA, Lantern Books, New York, 2011, p.169.

≪The Road to Enlightenment≫
On the afternoon of 23 of March 1981, I sat back in the warm spring sunshine and reflected on my life up to then and including the period at university, and wondered what I should do in the future. The conclusion I came to was that I still wanted to establish myself as a philosopher by the age of thirty. I looked on it as my destiny.

But it was evident that I would not achieve this ambition unless I could become financially independent. In the meantime, my work at the trading organization would pay the bills and allow me to eat, and as I went on learning about society and continuing my private studies, I felt that a way to do what I intended would surely open for me.

Suddenly, I sensed an invisible presence with me in the room, and almost simultaneously understood by intuition that whatever it was it wished to communicate with me. I ran to get a pencil and some blank cards. My hand holding the pencil began to move as if it had a life of its own. On card after card it wrote the words "Good News," "Good News."

"Who are you?" I asked. My hand signed the name "Nikko." I was experiencing automatic writing under the control of Nikko, one of the six senior disciples of the thirteenth-century Buddhist saint Nichiren.

I was astounded. I had had no contact at all with the Nichiren sect of Buddhism. Furthermore, I was aware that "Good News" is equivalent to the word Gospel in Christian terminology, and I realized then that I had just experienced a sort of religious awakening. I was particularly astonished to have it made crystal clear to me while I was still alive that the spiritual world existed in reality, and that humans really did embody a life force that was immortal.

It was then that I grasped that my own spiritual eye had been starting to open over the previous two or three months. Strange flashes of light had occasionally disturbed me in my eyes; once or twice I had glimpsed a golden aura extending from the back of my head. Some time earlier, when I had paid a visit as a liberal arts student to the temple complex at Mount Koya, I had had a vision as I approached the inner sanctum: I saw myself in the future working with psychic forces. That had been the year, too, that I had come across a book by Masaharu Taniguchi called Shinsokan ("How to Visualize God") in a second-hand bookstore. One night I tried out the technique that he described, but when I put my hands together I was startled by the fiery current of energy that immediately flowed through them, and I never opened the book again. I thought his teaching was unoriginal anyway.

An even earlier spiritual experience came to me in my final year at elementary school. Lying in bed recuperating after suffering from a very high temperature, I engaged in astral travel several times. I visited heaven, and I also visited the Hell of Agonizing Cries in the lowest depths of hell. So, from an early age it was obvious that I possessed a strong predisposition toward, and sensitivity for, spiritual matters.

My contact with the spirit of Nikko did not last long, but I was soon contacted by Nichiren himself. He instructed me to "Love, nurture, and forgive," a form of teaching that was a precursor of the doctrine of the stages in the development of love that I was to formulate in later years (see Chapter Three). At the time, I wondered whether I had been a priest of the Nichiren sect in a previous life because the spirit of Nichiren continued to visit me regularly for at least a year afterward. Now, however, I am convinced that his purpose was to have me refute the false teachings since propagated in his name.

≪The Appearance of Christ and the Mission of Buddha≫
In June 1981, the spirit of Jesus Christ came down to tell me something absolutely extraordinary. He spoke with a trace of a foreign accent, but what he said was full of powerful sincerity and utter love. My father was with me at the time, and the presence of a spirit from so high a dimension left him bereft of speech. When a high spirit makes an earthly appearance in this way, it is within a numinous radiance that causes one's own body to become very warm, and the words it speaks are so filled with truth and light that one is moved to tears.

The following month, July, the secret repository of my subconscious was unlocked, and the hidden part of my consciousness— Gautama Siddhartha, Shakyamuni— began to talk to me in a mixture of Japanese and ancient Indian, urging me to take my destiny upon myself and to spread the word of Buddha.—He revealed to me that I was an incarnation of El Cantare, the focal consciousness of the Shakyamuni group1), and explained that it was my mission to be the salvation of all living creatures through the worldwide revelation of the Truth. The role of the Grand Nyorai Shakyamuni was twofold, he said. There is the side represented by the Nyorai Amida (the Savior), which consists of love, compassion, and faith. There is also that represented by the Nyorai Mahavairocana (the essence of Buddha), which is enlightenment, spiritual learning, and the secret knowledge of the spiritual domain. If the first aspect were to dominate within me, I would duly become a Grand Savior, but if the second aspect predominated I would instead become the Mahavairocana Buddha (the Great Enlightening), surpassing the Vairocana of the Garland or Mahavairocana Sutras.

I was utterly taken aback by it all. My upbringing had certainly been religious, and the existence of the spiritual realm I accepted as a proven fact. But this spiritual experience was so overpowering, and the scope of the mission set for me so enormous, that I could not conceal my shocked amazement. The only thing I understood at once was that I was a reincarnation of Buddha, and that it was to be up to me to reorganize the high spirits in heaven while also integrating all the various religions on Earth to create a new world religion. It was for me to gather all the peoples of the world into this new faith, to see to the development of a new civilization, and so herald the advent of a new age for the world.

(text partly omitted)

I now have to tell all the people in the world about the incarnation from the ninth dimension of El Cantare, and about His mission on Earth. It is the Coming, the Advent, the appearance on Earth of the highest Buddha, the supreme Savior. The world is in the process of undergoing purification, and through acceptance of El Cantare humanity can achieve the highest form of salvation.

Believe in El Cantare, and come gather round me.

Convey this message to all the people of the world. El Cantare is your Eternal Master.

Notes

1) The true earthly lives of the spirit of Shakyamuni Buddha are:

   1. La Mu   Mu
   2. Thoth   Atlantis
   3. Rient Arl Croud   ancient Inca Empire
   4. Ophealis   ancient Greece
   5. Hermes   ancient Greece
   6. Gautama Siddhartha ancient India
   7. Ryuho Okawa   present-day Japan

This constitutes the spiritual brotherhood of Shakyamuni, which exists in the ninth dimension.

3. Messages from Maitreya the Christ

Mr. Benjamin Creme, British artist and esotericist, had received 140 spiritual messages from Maitreya in heaven in the period from September 6, 1977 to May 27, 1982. Maitreya is said to be the ultimate Savior who comes to save mankind in the ultra far future.

Maitreya says in the messages that he himself is now dwelling among us to lead mankind and is strongly appealing to spread the fact of His Advent.

In the message number 10, he calls Jesus Christ "My Beloved Disciple, the Master Jesus". What kind of being is he who calls Jesus Christ "My Beloved Disciple, the Master Jesus"?

The group of Mr. Benjamin Creme is spread worldwide and is called Share International. The group is independent of Happy Science, the Japanese religious group founded by Master Ryuho OKAWA. Share International seems to have been searching for Maitreya in London for several decades since the last half of the 1970's. But until now they could not find Him.

I want to bring attention especially to the fact that the period Maitreya had sent the Messages includes the date March 23, 1981, on the day Master Ryuho OKAWA had spiritually awakened.

From the Messages, it is conjectured that Maitreya in heaven is the General Manager who had given Master Ryuho OKAWA the spiritual awakening.

If Jesus Christ and other great men in human history had given spiritual messages through Master OKAWA, then Maitreya who had spoken through Benjamin Creme must be none else than Master OKAWA.

The book is as follows.

"MESSAGES FROM MAITREYA THE CHRIST"
(1992, Benjamin Creme, London, Share International Foundation)

Here I want to present some Messages.

Message No. 1   September 6, 1977

My dear friends, it will not be long until you see my face.
When that time comes I shall take your hands in mine and
lead you to Him Whom we serve together.

My Manifestation is complete and accomplished.
I am, verily, in the world.

Soon you shall know Me, perhaps follow Me and love Me.
My Love flows ever through you all.
And that Love, which I hold for all mankind, has brought Me
here.
My brothers and sisters, My Return to the world is a signal
that the New Age, as you call it, has commenced.

In this coming time, I shall show you beauties and wonders
beyond your imaginings, but which are your birthright as
sons of God.

My children, My friends, I have come more quickly, perhaps,
than you expected.
But there is much to do, much that needs changing in the
world.
Many hunger and die, many suffer needlessly.

I come to change all that; to show you the way forward —

into a simpler, saner, happier life — together. No longer man against man, nation against nation, but together, as brothers, shall we go forth into the New Country.

And those who are ready shall see the Father's face.

May the Divine Love and Light and Power of the One God be now manifest within your hearts and minds.

May this Light and Love and Power lead you to seek That which dwells always in your heart's centre.

Find That, and make It manifest.

Maitreya says that He returned to this world because of His Love for mankind, to remove sufferings and to make the New Age.

Message No. 6   October 11, 1977

Good evening, My dear friends.
Once again, I have the pleasure of speaking to you in this way.

Very little time indeed now separates Me from you, in full vision.
Mankind will see Me very soon.

And, if they follow Me, I shall lead them forward into the future which awaits them:
a future bathed in the light of Truth, of Harmony, and Love.

My friends, I would ask you to help Me, to take upon yourselves a share of the burden of preparation.
If you can accept that I am here, make known this fact wherever you find a listener.

It may be that you will see Me without knowing Me.
It may be that you will walk the other way.

But, if this be so, you will forfeit a treasure unlike that which you might build in a thousand lifetimes.

Make it your task to tell men that I am here, that I am working for them, for their future, for the future of all men and all things in the world.

Make known My Presence among you, and be delivered of all that is useless in the past.

Make known My Presence, and be assured that My Love will flow through you and light a path before you for your brothers and sisters.
Do this work and help them and Me.

My task is but beginning.
When completed, I shall look back on this time as one of kindling Light in the hearts of the few who sought to serve their brothers.
May you be one of them.

My heartfelt Love flows to you all.

May the Divine Light and Love and Power of the One God be now manifest within your hearts and minds.
May this manifestation lead you to seek That which lies hidden but ever ready to shine forth.
Find That and know God.

Maitreya says that " if you walk to the other way, you will lose a treasure unlike that which you might build in a thousand lifetimes ".

The importance of these Messages is understood. From the word "a thousand lifetimes", Maitreya's thought is similar to Buddhism.

3. Messages from Maitreya the Christ

Message No. 10   November 8, 1977

I am among you once more, My dear friends.

I come to tell you that you will see Me very soon, each in his own way.
Those who look for Me in terms of My Beloved Disciple, the Master Jesus, will find His qualities in Me.
Those who look for Me as a Teacher are nearer the mark, for that is what I am.
Those who search for signs will find them, but My method of manifestation is more simple.

Nothing separates you from Me, and soon many will realise this.
I am with you and in you.
I seek to express That which I am through you; for this I come.

Many will follow Me and see Me as their Guide.
Many will know Me not.
My aim is to enter into the life of all men and, through them, change that life.
Be ready to see Me soon.
Be ready to hear My words,
to follow My thoughts,
to heed My Plea.

I am the Stranger at the Gate.
I am the One Who knocks.
I am the One Who will not go away.
I am your Friend.
I am your Hope.
I am your Shield.
I am your Love.
I am All in All.

Take Me into yourselves, and let Me work through you.
Make Me part of yourselves, and show Me to the world.
Allow Me to manifest through you, and know God.

May the Divine Light and Love and Power of the One and Holy God be now manifest within your hearts and minds.
May this manifestation lead you to know that God dwells silently, now and forever, within you all.

   Maitreya calls Jesus Christ "My Beloved Disciple". Maitreya is in such a position that He guides Jesus Christ.

3. Messages from Maitreya the Christ

Message No. 17   **February 14, 1978**

Good evening, My dear friends, I am happy to be with you once more in this way.

Soon My Appearance will be known to many and My Teaching will have begun.
Mankind will be faced by Me with two lines of action; on their decision rests the future of this world.
I will show them that the only possible choice is through sharing and mutual interdependence.
By this means, man will come into that state of awareness of himself and his purpose which will lead him to the feet of God.
The other way is too terrible to contemplate, for it would mean the annihilation of all lifestreams on this Earth.

Man has the future in his hands.
Weigh well, oh men, and if you choose as true men would, I may lead you into the Light of your divine inheritance.
Make your choice well, and let Me lead.
Make your choice well, and be assured of My continuing succour.
Make your choice well, My brothers, and be delivered of all that holds you in limitation.

My Army is on the move, is marching bravely into the future.

Join those who already fight on the side of Light, on the side of Truth, of Freedom and Justice.
Join My Vanguard and show the way for your brothers.

Many there are who sense that I am here, yet speak not.
Why hold this knowledge to yourself when your brothers cry for light, for wisdom, and help?
Allow them, too, to share in the joy of the Promise which I bring.
Tell them, My friends, that you believe that Maitreya has come; that the Load of Love is here; that the Son of Man walks again among His brothers.
Tell them that soon My face will be seen, My words will be heard; and in the seeing and the hearing, they are tested and known.

May the Divine Light and Love and Power of the One Most Holy God be now manifest within your hearts and minds.
May this manifestation lead you to seek and to find that Divine Source from which you came.

Maitreya says that there are but two paths of which mankind must choose and if mankind chooses the wrong path, all lifestreams would be annihilated. This statement coincides with the Mosaic word that the present day is facing crisis.

3. Messages from Maitreya the Christ

Message No. 73   **June 19, 1979**

My dear ones, it is with joy that I take this further opportunity to speak to you in this manner.

My joy likewise is enlarged when I see within you the Spirit of Love manifesting.
This brings to My heart a joy which you cannot know.
Men think of Myself and My Brothers in isolation.
This, My friends, is far from the truth.
Each tremor of Love felt within your heart is registered in mine.
This is the simple truth of our relationship.
Know then, My friends, how great is the joy I feel when I sense your expectation, your release from fear, and know your trust.

My way is being prepared.
Make it your task, My brothers and sisters, to share this burden.
Create around you the atmosphere of trust and hope into which I soon may enter.
Believe Me, My friends, this is a Great Work indeed.
Much depends on the creation of this pool of Trust, this atmosphere of hope.

When I tell you that My feet have already walked the

pavements of your cities, this, My friends, is the truth.
Men are known to Me in the fullest sense:
I know their hopes and fears.
I know their longings and yearnings.
I know their aspiration for good.
Upon all of this I rely.

Make it your avowed task to aid Me in My coming work.
May it be that you become channels for My Love.
In this way shall you fulfil your destiny, too.

May the Divine Light and Love and Power of the One Most Holy God be now manifest within your hearts and minds.
May this manifestation lead you to see yourselves as My agents.

Maitreya says that His feet have already walked on the pavements of our cities. It means in reality Maitreya the Savior is dwelling in our midst. And also He says that we must make it our task to share His burden.

Finally I want to present the last Message.

3. Messages from Maitreya the Christ

Message No. 140   May 27, 1982

My dear friends, I am happy to be with you once again, and to give you this last communication in this way.

It has been My intention to reveal Myself at the earliest possible moment, to brook no delay, and to come before the world as your Friend and Teacher.
Much depends on My immediate discovery, for in this way can I help you to save your world.
I am here to aid and teach, to show you the path to the future, and to reveal you to each other as Gods.

I am sure you realise that much depends on the actions of men in the coming years.
All the world knows this.
All the world stands in fear.
Nevertheless, there is a growing sense of hope, a likelihood of change, a response to My Presence, creating thus a point of stillness in the tension.

Hopes now run high for My Appearance.
Gladly would I present Myself to the people.
Look for Me then, and find Me waiting.

Search for Me then, and grasp My hand.

I need your help to come before you, to bless this world and teach, to show men that the way forward is simple, requires only the acceptance of Justice and Freedom, Sharing and Love.

These aspects are already within you and need only to be evoked by Me.

Christ is here, My friends.
The Avatar has come.
Your Brother walks among you.
My Mission begins.
Know Me soon and help your brothers to know Me.
Take My hand and let Me lead you to God.

May the Divine Light and Love and Power of the One Most Holy God be now manifest within your hearts and minds.
May this manifestation lead you quickly to see your roles in this heroic time.

Maitreya the Savior says that He is now really among us, urges us to find Him quickly and He says also that the future of mankind depends on the actions of mankind.

Here I have presented some Messages from Maitreya the Christ. Is it only I who feels that these messages are full of Dignity and Kindness and Nobleness? I think these qualities indicate also that these messages had been given from El Cantare in Heaven.

If the Messages from Maitreya the Christ is true and Maitreya is not El Cantare in Heaven, then it must be logically concluded that there are two Messiahs who exceed Jesus Christ that are dwelling on Earth now in the same age. This creates a conflict that is not easy to accept. So Maitreya in Heaven who had sent 140 Messages is strongly conjectured to be El Cantare in Heaven.

4. The Prophecies of Michel Nostradamus

I have taken up here four verses related to the grand Messiah out of the original French prophecies of Michel Nostradamus and tried to interpret these. It can be seen that quite different interpretations from conventional ones could be made. French original verses were referred from the following book.

"The Complete Prophecies of NOSTRADAMUS", Translated, Edited, and Interpreted by HENRY C.ROBERTS, NEW REVISED EDITION Re-edited by Lee Roberts Amsterdam and Harvey Amsterdam, Published by NOSTRADAMUS CO., NEW YORK, ISBN 0-517-54956-5

Following is the famous the year 1999 verse.

CENTURY 10 No. 72

L'an mil neuf cens nonante neuf sept mois,
Du ciel viendra un grand Roy d'effrayeur,
Resusciter le grand Roy d'Angolmois,
Avan apres, Mars regner par bon heur.

The first line can be interpreted as "In the year 1999, the seventh month".

"Du ciel" of the second line means "From the sky" but it can also be interpreted as "From Heaven". Next "viendra" means "would come" but it can also be interpreted as "would descend". Next "un grand Roy d'effrayeur" can be interpreted as "one great tremendous King". So, the second line can be interpreted as " From Heaven, one great tremendous King would descend ".

"Angolmois" of the third line is interpreted commonly as the anagram of "Mongolias" that means "Mongolian people". It may also be interpreted as "Eastern Oriental", so "le grand Roy d'Angolmois" may be "Eastern Oriental great King". And I think He would be Buddha. The word "Resusciter" is not found in modern French but it is commonly interpreted as "to restore". So the third line can be interpreted as
" To restore the great King of Mongolias (Buddha) "

The fourth line can be interpreted as

" Before and after, Mars shall reign for human happiness ".

Mars is the symbol of military force. The present day is the age of nuclear deterrent force. It cannot be true peace.

So, it would not be right to interpret this verse as "From the sky, an awful great King will fall on Earth" as Japanese interpreter Mr. Ben Goto had made in his book. His interpretation is unnatural. Finally, this verse can be interpreted as follows.

In the year 1999, in the seventh month,
From Heaven, one great tremendous King would descend,
To restore the great King of Mongolias (Buddha),
Before and after, Mars shall reign for human happiness.

So, this verse is not only an awful prophecy but is a hopeful one that tells us of the Advent of the Grand Messiah. The verses of Nostradamus are difficult to interpret before the event happens, so we cannot fault Mr. Ben Goto.

By the way, Master OKAWA was born on July 7, 1956. And in the period at the end of the millennium including the year 1999, in Japanese religious group Happy Science, the Birthday Festival of Master OKAWA had been taking place in July every year. It is a festival celebrating the Advent of Grand Messiah El Cantare.

In the end, this verse can be smoothly interpreted if we interpret that this verse is predicting the Advent of Lord El Cantare Master OKAWA at the end of the millennium.

Following verse is also interesting.

CENTURY 10 No. 75

Tant attendu ne reviendra jamais,
Dedans l'Europe, en Asie apparoistra,
Un de la ligue yssu du grand Hermes,
Et sur tous Roy des Orients coistra.

The first line and the second line can be interpreted as follows.

" He who was very expected would never appear in Europe, but He would appear in Asia, "

The third line and the forth line can be interpreted as follows.

" He is one of the members of the group stemming from the great Hermes, And He shall exceed all the Kings of Orient. "

The earthly lives of Master OKAWA is shown in "section 2. Ryuho OKAWA Spiritual Messages". Hermes is one of Master OKAWA's spiritual brothers. Thus Hermes is one of the members of the El Cantare soul group. The word Hermes appears directly in the prophecy. It is a terrible coincidence.

The word Orient means east of Europe, so it may include Palestine, the Middle East, India and China. So, "all the Kings of Orient" would be Jesus Christ, Shakyamuni and Confucius and others. The word "King" is used as "Messiah" in the verse of the year 1999 too.

By the way, as was mentioned in "section 3. Messages from Maitreya the Christ", the worldwide group Share International founded by Mr. Benjamin Creme has been searching for the Messiah in London for several decades since the latter half of the 1970's. So, the first and the second lines "He who was very expected would never appear in Europe" can be interpreted as that the group would extensively search for the Grand Messiah in Europe but He would never be found in Europe. Maitreya the Christ had said in His messages that He would appear on Earth forthwith. So, it would be unnatural if He does not appear after even several decades had passed from His Messages. In the second line, as it is said that He would appear in Asia, if Master OKAWA had made the Advent as Grand Messiah in Japan, it can consistently be understood. Finally, this verse can be interpreted as follows.

He who was very expected would never appear
In Europe, but He would appear in Asia,
He is the one of the soul brothers of great Hermes,
And He shall exceed all the Kings of Orient.

Whereas the verse of the year 1999 is predicting the time of the Advent, this verse is thought to be predicting the place of the Advent. And these verses are placed nearer to each other, one is No. 10.72 and another is No. 10.75, so these verses seem to have a close relationship.

He who descends at the end of the 20th century and He who descends in Asia and He who revives Mongolias Great King (Buddha) and He who is the soul brother of Great Hermes is none other than Master OKAWA. However extensively we search for Him throughout the world, there is no one but Master OKAWA who matches Him. It would be a logical conclusion that Master OKAWA is just Him whom Nostradamus predicted as the Grand Messiah.

Well, the following verse is also interesting.

CENTURY 5 No. 53

La loy de Sol, & Venus contendans,
Apparopriant l'esprit de prophetie,
Ne l'un ne l'autre ne seront entendans,
Par Sol tiendra la loy du grand Messie.

This verse can be interpreted as follows.

The Law of the Sun and the Law of the Venus would compete,
Using the spirit of prophecy,
Though both parties do not heed each other,
The Law of the Grand Messiah would be held by the Sun.

"THE LAWS OF THE SUN" is the title of Master OKAWA's famous book, which is the most basic text of the Japanese religious group Happy Science. The title appears directly in the prophecy. It is a terrible coincidence.

The Sun in the forth line seems to mean the book "THE LAWS OF THE SUN" and also Japan. After Nostradamus, no one but Master OKAWA had written a book entitled "The Law of the Sun", and from this fact too it is presumed strongly that Master OKAWA is the Grand Messiah.

"The Law of the Venus" is difficult to interpret but is conjectured to be the law that the group of Benjamin Creme preaches because of the following reasons. Up to the present, both groups have not heeded each other.

The group that preaches "The Law of the Venus" must be spiritual because Nostradamus says they would be "Using the spirit of prophecy". And also that group must be worldwide because Nostradamus dares to mention them in his prophecy placing it side by side with "The Law of the Sun". If they would be a local phenomenon, Nostradamus would not have mentioned them. The group of Benjamin Creme satisfies these conditions.

Moreover Mr. Benjamin Creme is said to be an esotericist. The word "esoteric" means inner directed and it implies the "closed", the "mysterious", even the "mystique of the female", the "goddess" and "Venus". On the other hand the word "exoteric", which stands in contrast to the word "esoteric", means outer directed and it implies the "open", the "universal", "universalism", even the "Messiah" and the "Sun".

Now, I want to present the last verse related to the Grand Messiah.

CENTURY 1 No. 48

Vingt ans du regne de la lune passez,
Sept mil ans autre tiendra sa monarchie,
Quand le soleil prendra ses jours laissez,
Lors accomplit a fine ma Prophecie.

This verse is interpreted as follows. (by Henry Roberts)

Twenty years of the reign of the moon having passed,
Seven thousand years another shall hold his monarchy,
When the sun shall resume his days past,
Then is fulfilled and ends my prophecy.

The interpretation of this verse is difficult. The word "soleil (sun)" in the third line can be thought as the book "THE LAWS OF THE SUN" and also Japan. From the phrase "my prophecy is fulfilled and ends", this verse can be regarded as the last prophecy of Nostradamus. So it is thought that the prophecy of the Advent of the Grand Messiah has great importance in his prophecies.

As presented thus far, the four prophecies of Nostradamus can be understood as a strong external evidence of the Grand Messiah El Cantare Master Ryuho OKAWA.

Here, I want to present a part of a book in which Master OKAWA had mentioned Nostradamus.

"The Origin of Youth", Ryuho OKAWA, IRH press, October 2007, P156
(Translated from Japanese to English by K.Kakoi)

"THE LAWS OF THE SUN" predicted by Nostradamus

In the last half of the 20th century, many kinds of books on the prophecies of Nostradamus had appeared and some persons had mentioned about it. Happy Science had also for a time published some books on Nostradamus and I had mentioned them in some of preaches.

Because already the 20th century had passed and we are now in the 21st century, many people may think that all of his prophecies had failed. But I do not feel that his prophecies had failed. The reason is as follows.

I had written a book entitled "THE LAWS OF THE SUN" in the year 1986 by so called revelational automatic writing. The title was not thought up by me, but it first appeared when I had written the manuscript by automatic writing. Then I had written "THE GOLDEN LAWS" in the same year 1986 by automatic writing.

In those days, I knew that there were these terrifying prophecies of Nostradamus, but I did not know of its details.

And after I had written "THE LAWS OF THE SUN" and "THE GOLDEN LAWS", I happened to read something about Nostradamus and I found a description that "Hermes would revive in the eastern country and He would bring prosperity".

There had been no relations between the description and my statement in the book "THE GOLDEN LAWS" that "Hermes is a part of Buddha consciousness and I had been Hermes in past life". Independent of the description, I had spiritually awakened that I am the rebirth of Hermes so I had written it in "THE GOLDEN LAWS".

I did not write my books after I had read the Nostradamus items but in fact I found the description after I had written my books.

Furthermore, in the Nostradamus book it is written that "The Laws of the Sun shall be preached. When the Laws of the Sun had been preached, my prophecies shall be finished".

"The Law of the Sun" had never been written by anyone except for me in the past four hundred years after Nostradamus. And when I had written my book "THE LAWS OF THE SUN", the title had firstly appeared at the automatic writing as I stated above. So I had never been told that you must write the book according to the prophecies of Nostradamus from four hundred years ago. At that moment, I had no knowledge at all that there were such prophecies since four hundred years ago.

And when I sent the manuscript of "THE LAWS OF THE SUN" to the publisher who had been publishing my spiritual messages, I was told that this book could not be published. The publisher thought that they could publish the spiritual messages, but with the title "THE LAWS OF THE SUN", the implication would be that the author is claiming its contents. The president of the publisher said to me that they would ask me to change the title to "The Spiritual Messages from Shakyamuni" from "THE LAWS OF THE SUN" so that they can publish it. He said that that's too bad because if the title was "The Spiritual Messages from Shakyamuni" then they could publish it. They furthermore said that if the title is "The Spiritual Messages from Shakyamuni", then people would believe it. But if the title implies that they are the author's thought, then people would not believe it, so I must not express my own thoughts.

So the manuscript of "THE LAWS OF THE SUN" had never been read through by the staff and it had been left alone for months. At that time, I had sent the manuscript without a copy. So I said, "If you can not publish, I want it returned". And after it was returned, I published it with another publisher. Now the book is published from IRH press.

It may have seemed like cheap things because I had made the manuscript of "THE LAWS OF THE SUN" by automatic writing on manuscript papers, and even if it was published, it would never be read by people. The president who had not published "THE LAWS OF THE SUN" could not have thought that the book shall come to have such a great influence.

I myself had had the recognition that this book has relevance to all of mankind and is of great importance, so I strongly wanted to publish it and felt great impatience. For this reason, I had published this book from another publisher.

Nostradamus had made prophecies four hundred years ago on the prosperity brought by Hermes and on "THE LAWS OF THE SUN" and he also said that after these prophecies had been fulfilled, his mission would end.

Nostradamus of four hundred years ago would not only be a prophet who only foresees the future, but he would be a prophet who keeps the words from God for the Person who shall come later, who shall appear at the end of the millennium. And he said also that after he had passed the baton to the predicted Person, he would have no other missions to be fulfilled.

A part of the verses of Nostradamus had been scattered and lost, so the verses may not be complete. But the two prophecies claim that Hermes would be revived and that He would bring new prosperity and that "THE LAWS OF THE SUN" would be advocated had been kept for four hundred years. On this issue, Heaven moved brilliantly and I had come into the world and wrote "THE LAWS OF THE SUN".

So these two prophecies would have relations to the plan of Heaven. It seems that in Heaven since the days of Nostradamus there had been a big plan and a promise that at the turning point from the 20th century to the 21st century, a new civilization would emerge and commence.

5. Miracles within the Happy Science

Now many miracles are reported in the religious group Happy Science. There are many incidents where doctors were astonished. For example, there is a man who had come back from an incurable disease, who had recovered in short time completely from cerebral contusion caused by a traffic accident. Of these incidents, please refer to the monthly magazines or booklets of the Happy Science.

Above all, to our surprise, besides Master OKAWA there are some channelers who can receive spiritual messages. There are no spirits whether they may be angels or evil spirits whom Master OKAWA cannot summon. In fact, "Ryuho OKAWA Spiritual Message Corrections" is composed of the messages from Jesus Christ and other great persons in human history.

In some cases, Master OKAWA lets an evil spirit descend in a channeler and through him makes the evil spirit talk. Any evil spirit summoned in front of Master OKAWA is his true nature disclosed. The sight of an evil spirit talking is full of realism. The situation is recorded on videotapes at the facilities of Happy Science and anyone can see and listen to it at the Happy Science branch facilities.

Sometimes Master OKAWA summons a spirit into Him from the spiritual world and lets the spirit talk through Him. And thereafter He sends the spirit into another channeler and lets the spirit continue his talk through the channeler. This phenomenon cannot be explained unless the spirit in the spiritual world is really talking through Master OKAWA and the channeler.

And sometimes conversations happen between Master OKAWA and the channeler using ancient language of which age is uncertain but is the language of the past life of the channeler. That is Glossolalia in the Bible. If the Glossolalia is the language of the past life of the channeler, it would be an evidence of reincarnation.

Additionally, there is another miraculous phenomenon. Many UFOs had appeared far up in the sky over the assembly hall of Yokohama Arena where the El Cantare festival had been held on December 4, 2010. In the speech entitled "An Introduction to World Religion — Paradigm Shift to Earthman", Master OKAWA said that soon interactions with space brothers would commence. After the speech, outside of the main hall, thousands of listeners had witnessed many UFOs far up in the sky. This phenomenon seems to be the precursor of phenomena that shall occur in future time.

Here I want to quote a blog of Mr. Naofumi Sato who was the Happiness Realization Party Publications Office Director in December 4, 2010.
http://satonaofumi.blog68.fc2.com/blog-entry-240.html
(Translated from Japanese to English by K.Kakoi)

5. Miracles within the Happy Science

December 4, 2010. Large group of UFOs appeared in the sky over the assembly hall Yokohama Arena where Happy Science El Cantare festival had been held

On December 4, the El Cantare festival that is one of two big festivals of Happy Science had been held. On that day, 10,000 people had assembled in the main assembly hall Yokohama Arena and other peoples had assembled in 3,000 domestic and international assembly halls where satellite relay had been offered. And the festival became a big event of 100,000 peoples in all.

Mr. Tatsuro KINJO also had hurried to the main hall from Okinawa who had bravely fought through the Okinawa gubernatorial election, and expressed his appreciation and thanked all the supporters through the whole country.

In the festival, from Master OKAWA, the speech entitled "An Introduction to World Religion — Paradigm Shift to Earthman" had been given and taught that in loves there is a love to lead a person, lead him to the true faith and also had been taught of the importance of spreading faith and mission work.
Furthermore, hereafter facing a genuine space age, considering the interactions with 20 or more types of space brothers who are said to have come to Earth now, Master OKAWA had given us a magnificent and large scaled speech

that it is the work of El Cantare to resolve the Laws of the Universe that reaches from faith view to cosmology.

After the festival, outside of the main hall, many people were stopping and pointing to the sky. So I too joined them in hurry
looked up and was astonished!
I saw there in the clear sky, many strange flying objects drifting and moving in irregular passes with some silver shine!! In a fluster, I had taken a digital camera out and took pictures by 7 times zoom mode which are the two pictures shown in the following page.

Looking closely, they seemed to be changing in the shape of boomerangs or to squares and also changing the color to blue or orange.

It seemed really that hearing the speech of Master OKAWA, they appealed their existence. So I in haste uploaded this report.

Naofumi Sato.

5. Miracles within the Happy Science

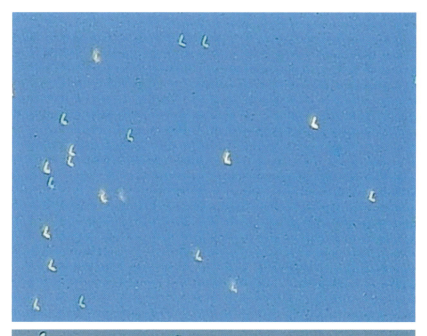

6. Conclusion

Ryuho OKAWA Grand Messiah hypothesis was presented here to consistently explain the following four independent phenomena.

① Ryuho OKAWA Spiritual Messages
② Messages from Maitreya the Christ
③ The Prophecies of Michel Nostradamus
④ Miracles within the Happy Science

These four phenomena are combined deeply and tightly with each other. According to Francis Bacon's expression, the bays and capes are deeply corresponding to each other like a jigsaw puzzle which can never be thought to be there by chance. There is no other hypothesis that can explain these phenomena consistently except for the Ryuho OKAWA Grand Messiah hypothesis.

The hypothesis may seem very extraordinary because it proclaims that Master OKAWA is the Grand Messiah who came to save the current world and who excels above even Jesus Christ.

But the logical conclusion is strong. A theorem of mathematics is correct to the ends of the universe, to the ends of the spiritual world as long as the proof is correct.

The assertion that these four phenomena are only by chance

would be so strange as would be the assertion that the Multiple Simultaneous Terrorism acts in the United States of America happened on September 11, 2001 were caused by independent terrorist groups on the same day using the same means by chance.

These four phenomena would be Heavenly works, a Heavenly designed magnificent story.

Staring into the night sky, the magnificent story designed by Heaven could be seen spreading over the sky as far as the eye can see.

In physics, any hypotheses to explain phenomena are permitted. The more natural and simpler it is, the more the hypothesis is preferred. Newton's equation of motion is very simple but it explains a vast array of phenomena.

Ryuho OKAWA Grand Messiah hypothesis would from now on explain more and more phenomena and would be accepted by many peoples as firm knowledge and would become the hope of humanity, the lighthouse in the dark night.

It would make me glad if you would sincerely consider this article with an open mind and not to deny it easily because Maitreya says to do so means that you will forfeit a treasure unlike that which you might build in a thousand lifetimes. And also if you can accept this article, I would be glad if you can spread it to the ends of the world and make it reach to the hearts and minds of all the persons on this Earth.

Here I want to thank sincerely my friend Mr. Blackstone, a graduate of UCLA (philosophy), who helped me with my English text and offered significant interpretations on "the Law of the Venus" that appears in the prophecies of Nostradamus.

I thank you readers for reading through this article.

August, 2018
Kunihiko Kakoi

Author's Profile

Kunihiko Kakoi

Born in Osaka Japan, 1944. Graduated Kyoto University, faculty of
Science (Mathematics), dropped out of the master's course of Physics
at the same University. Dr. Eng. (Shinshu University) 1997. Mainly
engaged in R&D of numerical analysis of Tribology. At present,
President of TriboLogics corporation. Researcher of religious group
Happy Science. Lecturer of Happy Science University.

大川隆法大救世主仮説 英語版

2018 年 8 月　初版第 1 刷

著　者：梛井邦彦

発行所：株式会社トラ研
　　　　住所：〒206-0041
　　　　東京都多摩市愛宕 1-630-12
　　　　TEL：(042)316-9731　FAX：(042)316-9753
　　　　E-mail:info@tribology.co.jp
　　　　http://www.tribology.co.jp

印刷・製本：三美印刷株式会社

©Kunihiko Kakoi 2018, Printed in Japan, 検印省略
ISBN978-4-904176-04-7